Healing

Works in this series include:

The Nature of The Soul

Creative Thinking

The Soul and Its Instrument
(The Path of Initiation, Vol. III)

The Disciple and Economy

Leadership Training

Ashramic Projections

The Path of Initiation, Vols. I & II
(a.k.a. Introduction to the Path of Initiation)

Healing

Applied Wisdom
(Scheduled for publication in 2005)

These works are available through Wisdom
Impressions.

II

Healing

By Lucille Cedercrans

Wisdom Impressions
Whittier, CA

Healing

by Lucille Cedercrans

First edition, 2005

Wisdom Impressions is a group of practitioners of The Wisdom. Our purpose is to help create the appearance, support the teaching, and facilitate the distribution of The Wisdom.

Wisdom Impressions
PO Box 130003
Roseville, MN 55113

IV

The Great Invocation

From the point of Light within the Mind of God
Let light stream forth into the minds of men.
Let Light descend on Earth.

From the point of Love within the Heart of God
Let love stream forth into the hearts of men.
May Christ return to Earth.

From the center where the Will of God is known
Let purpose guide the little wills of men —
The purpose which the Masters know and serve.

From the center which we call the race of men
Let the Plan of Love and Light work out
And may it seal the door where evil dwells.

Let Light and Love and Power restore the Plan on Earth.

"The above Invocation or Prayer does not belong to any person or group but to all Humanity. The beauty and the strength of this Invocation lies in its simplicity, and in its expression of certain central truths which all men, innately and normally accept—the truth of the existence of a basic Intelligence to Whom we vaguely give the name of God; the truth that behind all outer seeming, the motivating power of the universe is Love; the truth that a great Individuality came to earth, called by Christians, the Christ, and embodied that love so that we could understand; the truth that both love and intelligence are effects of what is called the Will of God; and finally the self-evident truth that only through *humanity* itself can the Divine Plan work out."

Alice A. Bailey

VI

Foreword

The following work begins with a five lesson course on Healing (which we originally published as a booklet). This course has here been expanded with three new lessons—including "Developing Your Healing Capacities", "Therapy", and "Diet"—plus six additional healing techniques.

The resulting work may be summed up in the following:

"Every disciple, to a greater or lesser degree, develops his own particular method of healing. You combine Second and Seventh Ray techniques as you develop your particular potential along this line. That healing potential is more predominant with a Second Ray disciple than with some of the others in the group. You have the potential of a healer and can develop this potential via an act of the will which focuses the attention upon it, if you so choose. That you will develop along this line anyway is true. The type of vision is natural for you to develop because of the particular emphasis placed in past incarnations upon the development and use of the third eye. This, then, is a natural and normal expression for you."

R/Lucille

Sincerely,

Wisdom Impressions

April, 2005

VIII

Table of Contents

"In recognition of, and cooperation with this activity of the Soul, a *new thought-form presentation of The Wisdom* has been created and placed in availability for those who seek it. It can be contacted as an abstraction via the activity of meditation, and must then be translated into a concrete form by the one who meditates.

"This series of instructions is an interpretation of that new thought-form and has been written in an effort to aid man in the search for his Soul.

"For those who seek authority behind the written word, the truth of this text must be proven via its application. A formulated concept is of value only if it can be worked out as a living truth within the life and affairs of Humanity. Therefore do not look to the source of this teaching for its authenticity, but to the application of it within your own life and affairs."

The Nature of The Soul, pp. 3 - 4

X

Lesson 1

The State of Consciousness
Necessary to Healing

This series of instructions is being written for all of those aspirants upon the Path of Initiation who have definitely felt the call of service and are seeking sufficient knowledge with which to answer that call. They are those whose feet are well placed upon the Path and whose next step forward is into the realm of discipleship. This stage of evolution presupposes a certain unfoldment of Soul consciousness, which I shall endeavor to explain.

1. Right motive.

The aspirant has traveled the path of experience sufficiently long to realize his essential relation to all other persons. He is a Soul, related to all other Souls, being therefore, a brother of all men.

He recognizes the fact that he can have no purpose, no motive, and no goal, which is not the motive, purpose, and goal of all men. It would be impossible for him to acquire anything for the separated self, for his very nature demands that he share that which he is with his brothers. He has had a glimpse into the Kingdom of Heaven, he senses the beauty of the Divine Plan, he has, in a greater or lesser degree, achieved rapport with the Soul of all things. All of this serves to stimulate his aspiration to the Soul, but that aspiration is characterized by its inclusiveness. He aspires for all men, realizing that he cannot know complete peace until it has been attained by the entire human family.

Could a man be content to eat his fill and see his brothers in need of food?

2. Selflessness.

As a result of his realization of brotherhood, the disciple is enabled to put all thoughts of self aside in order to serve. He, as a separated personality, becomes a nonentity as he loses himself in service to the Plan. The petty desires, selfish aims, the dissatisfactions are not known by him. His vision sees so much farther and includes that which is so much greater, that things of the personality become insignificant in comparison, and are eventually forgotten in service. To others it would appear that his entire life is a great sacrifice, but to his consciousness, service itself is its own reward.

My friends, look beyond the outer appearance, observe the beauty and the perfection of God's Plan on earth. Realize that you are a part of that Plan and the unhappiness, the constant strife and turmoil, will drop from you as an old worn out cloak. Yours will be the joy, the inner peace, and the strength of the divine Soul in action!

3. Sensitiveness to world need.

This, of course, is dependent upon many factors: the type and quality of the equipment with which the aspirant must work, his karmic obligations, etc. It is also dependent upon the degree of discrimination he has developed. He must be able to discriminate between true world need and astral glamour. It is this discrimination which differentiates the true disciple from the would-be disciple. Many of the difficulties apparent in the world today are a direct result of individuals and groups registering what they think is world need. The

Chapter 1

"isms", separative organizations, etc., are manifestations of sensitiveness without discrimination.

The true disciple is non-violent, non-critical, all-inclusive in his recognition of brothers, ever loving, kind and considerate. His is not the activity of destruction, for he knows that destruction is an inner activity. That which is no longer included in God's Plan destroys itself. This is a basic law and must be realized before a true field of service can be entered. There are no disciples who are concerned with the work of conscious destruction. The concept of such a work is astral glamour, a distortion of true need. The disciple transmutes, synthesizes, and builds. He leaves such things as destruction to the Universal Law and is not blinded by this type of glamour.

I shall speak here of vision, for it is this attribute which renders the disciple sensitive to world need. It is intuitive vision which enables the disciple to differentiate the real from the unreal, the important from the non or lesser important. Some call it understanding; it is a manifestation of Wisdom.

The disciple must have the capacity to pierce the clouds of illusion which hold the masses in ignorance, if he is to be of any service to humanity. What are some of these illusions? I shall point out those which are doing the greatest harm in the world today.

1. The illusion of evil.

This is a most difficult subject to discuss, for the concept of evil is so deep rooted, and of such immensity within the race mind; that the very attempt to reveal truth in this respect meets with powerful opposition.

Man is submerged in that which he himself has created. There is no such thing as evil except in the mind of man.

God created the manifest Universe, and it was good. He created man in his own image and gave him dominion over the fish of the sea, the birds of the heavens, and every living thing that moveth upon the earth. A study of those words and an application of the Law of Correspondence will bring much understanding to the aspirant.

The fish of the sea is, to the wise, symbolic and applies to the emotions of man found within the astral consciousness of the race. With his own astral body (sea) man creates those forms (fish) which go through an evolutionary process and eventually manifest within his life and affairs.

The birds of the air applies to the thoughts man accepts and embodies in the mental aspect of his own being. These thoughts (birds) take wing and pass from individual to individual within race mind consciousness (heavens).

Every living thing that moveth upon the earth applies to man's physical body and his manifesting environment.

There is, of course, a higher analogy which is seen by the initiate. I shall here give a hint in three words:

    a. Energy

    b. Moisture

    c. Substance

Man, who is created in the image and likeness of God, his parent, in turn creates within his own domain. God endowed him with creative energy and the seed of every living thing. Man applies this energy to the seed and brings into manifestation the results of his Wisdom, knowledge, and understanding. He is as yet a child, a half-God and his creative works reflect his growth or lack of growth.

At this time good and evil are the apparent result of man's evolution. Without knowledge of the Law he wields spiritual energy and in his ignorance creates that which he has called evil.

The devil of orthodox religion is but a thought-form, a powerful one, created by man, accepted in the astral consciousness of the race, and made manifest as a result of man's ignorance.

The disciple knows that the only devil he has to fear is that which he has created and given a home within himself.

The only hell he has to fear is that which results from his transgression of a law which he has created within his own mind, through lack of understanding Universal Law. Once man truly understands Universal Law, he cannot transgress it, for he has become that Law.

The aspirant has learned to understand good and evil in terms of Light and Dark Forces, but still his understanding is very limited and oft distorted. He is still under the influence of the illusion for he must still beware of Dark Forces and provide a protection for himself from them. To him they are very real, and in a sense he is correct, for they can and do apparently harm him. He is still identified with form and is then vulnerable to the conditions of the form.

The disciple, too, sees good and evil in terms of Dark and Light Forces, but his understanding is somewhat clearer than that of the aspirant. He has glimpsed the nature of karma and sees Darkness and Light as but the balance of the Universal Law. He accepts his karma, and through acceptance without fear adjusts those forces which manifest through him. He is unidentified with the form aspect and cannot therefore be harmed.

The initiate has achieved freedom from the concept of good and evil, even in terms of Light and Darkness, and is therefore removed from the illusion. His understanding can be only indicated to the uninitiated in those words of Paul, "To the Pure all things are pure."

The aspirant who is studying the art of healing, acquaints himself with the energies which are manifesting through the form. He learns to consider good and evil as right or wrong use of energy—right in the sense that a degree of perfection is achieved in form, wrong in the sense that the form is distorted and imperfect.

2. The illusion of importance or power.

This is another subject which is somewhat difficult to clarify, for average man and many beginners on the path are immersed in the illusion of importance.

This illusion is the result of mental polarization and is therefore experienced by almost everyone who begins to live and work in the realm of thought. The beginner has entered into a world in which he oft'times believes himself to be the originator and sole possessor of the answers to the problems of the world. He sees through much of the emotional distortion to the mental cause (which is often another distortion) and in so doing feels himself to be of more importance than those who are caught in the emotionalism so rampant today. He becomes the center of knowledge around which the universe revolves, and laying claim to that knowledge, sets out to make it law for his brothers.

The sense of power, completely distorted through lack of Wisdom on his part, lifts him even more in his own eyes into a position of importance. Others become little people over whom he (unconscious at first, and later consciously) exerts control, justifying himself in his belief of his own importance in the eyes of his God, which, by the way, is usually a reflected image of himself.

My friends, whatsoever you can reach of the Divine within yourselves, can also be reached within any other. Truth is universal; importance is universal; and none can lay claim to it above the other. Humility is a prerequisite to discipleship. It is a prerequisite to service. Jesus said, "Of myself I can do nothing; it is the Father within me which doeth all."[1] Think on this; it is important.

3. The illusion of inadequacy.

This is one of the most difficult of all illusions to pierce, for it often becomes a part of many an otherwise-capable disciple's equipment, rendering him useless to his brothers. It is one of the greatest kinds of selfishness evidenced by aspirants, and has been down through all the ages. If the aspirant would but realize that he cannot be inadequate since he is one with all men, that in thinking thus of himself he is entertaining one of the subtlest forms of separativeness. He is separating himself from his brothers, thinking of himself as being different, and in that very difference, important. Is not he too a Son of God? This particular illusion stems from many things; among them we find:

a. The fact that the aspirant has glimpsed a half vision of the Plan and not included himself in that Plan. It appears to him as something so much finer than he, that attainment of it is out of the realm of his possibilities.

---

[1] John 5: 30

b. The fact that he has observed the service of some one or more of his brothers, and out of a sense of competition does not measure up in his own eyes to their activities. My brother, while your brother's form of service may not be your own, your way complements his. Each has his place, each his path of service, and all make a whole. There are no competitors in service. There is only freedom and loving cooperation.

c. The fact that he is attached to past mistakes. He has tried to perform some form of service and failed. He has made many blunders and mistakes, and in looking back upon them, despises himself. I have never known of any disciple who has not experienced failure after failure. That is a part of the path, for experience is still the great teacher. To despise oneself is to deny God. To consider oneself inadequate to any task set before him is to deny God.

My brother, become detached from the past and let us have done with such foolishness.

Peace Be Unto You

Lesson 2

The State of Consciousness
of Those Who Ask for Healing

In our first lesson we considered in part the state of consciousness necessary to healing. In this lesson we shall consider the state of consciousness evidenced by those who generally ask for healing. They are many and varied, but we shall for the present consider those which are more predominant and those which the disciple is most likely to meet.

1. The probationer.

The greater percentage of probationers are suffering from dis-ease brought on largely as a result of precipitated karma, and it is often a result of incorrect experimentation. The disciple must first ascertain which of the two causes is responsible for the condition and act accordingly.

I would here briefly speak to you anent karma, for it is a concept very little understood and, therefore, the cause of much confusion. Karma is a term given to cover the Law of Action and Re-action. Every act must produce its re-action, and there you have it. Even that which I have termed incorrect experimentation produces karma, but it will be of an impersonal nature and therefore require somewhat different healing methods. The disciple must find the karmic cause responsible for the manifesting condition if he is to be of any real service to the brother in need. He must know the nature of the karma and the lesson to be learned thereby. I shall take up this subject of karma at greater length in our next lesson.

It must be remembered that a man is defined as a probationer when he has consciously or unconsciously approached the path and is in the process of deciding whether or not he is ready for that path. It may very well be that he is not ready, and if this is true it will be impossible for the disciple to effect a healing. The path itself is characterized by conscious aspiration, while the former stage is characterized by desire. The probationer is seeking, but he is motivated by selfish purpose. He represents a certain state of consciousness which is characterized by:

a. its unhappiness and suffering

b. its dissatisfaction with life in general

c. its lack of insight

d. its ability to sense something more worth-while than its own manifestations.

In other words, while such a one may be selfish, resentful, etc., he is usually aware of it and yearns for something finer. He it is who suffers from guilt complexes. This man will have many potentials, some of which he may or may not have partially developed. Always his relationships are incorrectly interpreted, his sense of values misplaced, and his ideals distorted.

It will depend upon the degree of distortion in regard to his ideals whether or not he is ready for the path, and this the disciple must ascertain. A responsibility? Yes, my brother, a very great responsibility when you realize you must not judge another, an apparent contradiction. You do not sit in judgment upon a brother, neither do you determine for him which path he must travel. It is up to you to let him be his own judge, to determine his own path, and then you must be content to abide by his decision. A very hard rule, and yet the disciple must live by it. See to it that you understand this rule and that you never force your convictions upon another.

Then how do you ascertain whether or not a probationer is ready to enter upon the path? By drawing him out, by letting him tell you, and this he will do as he reveals to you his ideals. The wish-life is actually the wish of the Soul reflected in the astral body. That wish-life or ideal may be such a distortion that it is still necessary for the Soul to taste further the path of experience. If the probationer is still so surrounded by the fog of ambition, pride, jealousy, resentment, etc., that his ideal is colored completely by them, then the disciple can only love him, bless him, and send him on his way, knowing that he will manifest his highest good. Until the disciple has learned to love impersonally without attachment, this is a difficult thing to do; for as he looks into the wish-life of the probationer, he will see and know the experience which must manifest as karma is precipitated.

When the disciple can see shining through that astral fog the clear light of understanding, even though it be but a spark, he knows the probationer will most likely accept a healing. Even though there be pride, ambition, etc., to a very great extent, if the ideal can be seen to reflect some understanding of basic values, then the disciple may proceed with the method indicated by the condition. With such methods we shall deal later.

2. The aspirant.

This state of consciousness is somewhat difficult to determine and usually difficult with which to deal. Often the aspirant himself is not fully aware that he is an aspirant, or more often a probationer thinks he is an aspirant. I have said in earlier lessons that not every student can be called an aspirant. An aspirant is one who has entered the Hall of Learning, and who is in the process of making what to him is the great sacrifice. He is deliberately and at seeming great cost, eliminating those personality traits which he can see tend to negate the expression of the Soul. His is the consciousness of duality, for the pairs of opposites provide for him the conflict. Let us list the most obvious opposites for better understanding:

Soul	Personality
Life	Death
Love	Hate
Fearlessness	Fear
Compassion	Cruelty
Harmlessness	Harmfullness
Selflessness	Selfishness
Humility	Pride
Right	Wrong

These, among many others, are the opposites with which the aspirant is faced. He is still primarily a personality, but he is aspiring to the Soul. His ideal is such that always he is faced with decision. He knows what for him constitutes right or wrong action, and between them he must choose. The desires of the personality are in constant conflict with his aspirations, and as a result he is a confused, bewildered student with much discomfort. No student can be called an aspirant unless he is putting himself through these disciplinary measures, honestly and with humility. He has consciously entered the path and is treading it. For a greater understanding of this stage of the path, I would advise you to study the *"Bhagavad Gita"*.

This state of consciousness is then characterized by:

a. its conflict with the pairs of opposites as the result of aspiration

b. its confusion as to motives, purposes, etc.

c. its sacrifices

d. its many fluctuations between ecstasy and depression, pain and pleasure, etc.

e. its psychosis.

Yes, all aspirants have either developed some definite psychosis or have psychotic tendencies. It can easily be deduced from the above that almost all disease experienced by the aspirant is psychological in nature. It is still necessary for the disciple to discover the karmic cause of the trouble, but he will use psycho-analytical methods to do so. With these we shall deal later.

3. The disciple.

This state of consciousness is easy for the true disciple to determine, for all disciples know and immediately recognize one another. Many times I have defined this state of consciousness for you; however for the sake of clarity I shall do so again.

A disciple is one who is conscious of himself as a Soul, and is aspiring to the Christ. He knows his identity, though he may not have a fully developed awareness of all that lies within the consciousness of the Soul.

He has recognized his service karma and is in the process

of adjusting it. All disciples serve; therefore, if one thinks of himself as a disciple and is not consciously engaged in service, he deludes himself. He may be nearing discipleship, but he has not as yet taken the initial step which gives him the rights and prerogatives of a disciple. Think on this, it is important.

A disciple is one who has entered the Hall of Wisdom and is absorbing Universal understanding. Both the head and the heart are utilized with equal facility. No disciple is ever on the head path or the heart path. The two paths have merged and the head and heart operate in unison for the betterment of all. The disciple is neither an occultist nor a mystic. This is the result of having been both as an aspirant. His knowledge, his understanding, is universal and is not confined to occultism or mysticism. Think on this, it is important.

There are various stages of discipleship which I will explain for your understanding. I shall speak in very broad and general outlines which can be filled in later as your understanding grows.

a. The new disciple.

The aspirant who has finally realized his identity, has recognized his need to serve, and is assuming his service karma, falls into this category. He has taken the First Initiation and is in the process of taking the Second. The personality is undergoing the purification which precedes Soul infusion. This purification necessarily covers a long period of time, during which the disciple is both in and out of incarnation. In a sense, the purification is but the beginning of that purification which is characteristic of the entire Path of Initiation. This one recognizes his service karma as the need to bring Divine Law and Order into his environment. For those who understand, he begins to work with the Seventh Ray of Law and Order, the synthesis of all the Rays reflected in form.

He is still very much concerned with the pairs of opposites, but his surface motives are more selfless. He disciplines himself more out of service to those around him than out of a desire to attainment. You will note, I stated surface motives. His pairs of opposites are much more subtle than those of the aspirant, for consciously he is motivated from a sincere desire to serve. At the same time he is confronted with a part of himself which he had not known existed. In the very midst of his love and humility, buried resentments, pride, etc., rear up to defeat him. He is forced to conquer them before he can continue along the path. His dis-eases are very similar to those of the aspirant, though usually of a more violent or deep-rooted nature.

  b. The second stage of discipleship.

This takes in that period where the disciple has conquered the most obvious part of his lower nature (the result of the present incarnation) with its natural distortions due to the culture, educational system, etc., and is now faced with the remnants of past incarnations. He will have found his Master, his subjective group of co-workers, his group on the physical plane, and his life work of service. Most of the environmental adjustments will have been made, and his concern will be with disciplining his instrument to that service chosen as the keynote of the present incarnation. He will spare the personality nothing in his efforts to carry out that work. He will have taken the Second Initiation and be in the process of taking the Third.

His dis-ease will be the result of faulty equipment, mistakes made in service, and incompleted karmic adjustments within the personality.

  c. The third stage of discipleship.

This stage covers that of the Initiate of the Third Degree

and higher. The disciple will be free from all environmental ties, well into that service karma which will be the key-note of the entire path, and closely associated with his Master and co-workers.

His dis-eases will be the result of national, racial, and world karma, faulty equipment, or the misdirection of energies received.

The methods of healing for all disciples will follow certain lines:

   a. directed meditation

   b. higher psycho-analytic procedure

   c. transmutation

   d. complete acceptance.

I shall clarify all of these methods in later lessons.

It stands to reason that disciples are easier to work with, in one sense, than those of a lesser evolution because they are capable of cooperation. They will work with the other, recognizing their very cooperation as a service, for their healing is a lesson to the brother helper. It is true, however, since the causes of their difficulties are more subtle, that their dis-ease is often of longer duration and sometimes impossible of cure in the present vehicle. Because their vision covers much more of eternity than that of the others, this is accepted with Wisdom and the service continues in spite of handicap.

Lesson 3

The Law of Karma

We come now to the Law of Karma, which is one of the basic laws governing evolution and therefore an understanding of it is vitally important to all aspirants and disciples. It is impossible, in the short space we have, to communicate all of the information necessary for such an understanding. However, I can give you some very basic teaching anent this subject, which will provide you with enough knowledge to co-operate with the Law. At a later date when there are more conscious disciples in the world and the work has progressed sufficiently, you will be provided with the necessary text books to cover the subject.

The Law of Karma, which is peculiarly related to the Cosmic Law of Economy, is (as I stated in the last lesson) the Law of Action and Re-action. Every act must produce its re-action; thus we have evolution of consciousness through experience in form.

An act is the deliberate focusing of the will by some creating agency. Behind every manifestation, there is intent or will, and it is this that determines the karmic content of the manifestation. If you can realize now that the act is not the manifestation, but rather it is that which causes manifestation, much will become clear that has heretofore been vague. For instance, the manifestation of murder is not the act of murder, but rather its reflection. The act took place in the mind and heart of the murderer when it was his will or intent to kill. The manifestation was the inevitable birth, in form, of that which had already been created. It is possible for the birth in form to be stillborn, premature and therefore a miscarriage, or deformed, but this makes little difference. The murderer committed the act as he willed the other to death and set into motion the Law of Karma.

Re-action is the last effect produced by the initial act, and is therefore the balancing or adjustment of energy displacement. Certain energies are directed to a definite destination when the act is committed. Those energies return with equal force, identical quality, and similar manifestation to their point of origin. See how beautifully and with what mathematical precision our Universe is made manifest? All is in perfect equilibrium at all times. If, when you see the manifestation of those things which are generally considered unpleasant, you could but realize that it is the balancing of energies, the adjustment of karma, resulting in growth for the human entity, life would become for you a thing of beauty and simplicity. Without this governing Law of Karma, our manifested Universe would fall apart, for there would be no balance.

When you meet with circumstances which are undesirable, learn to accept them with joy. They mean that your energies have been returned to you, and that certain of your karma is in the process of adjustment. The burden has actually been lessened rather than increased, and you are being freed from the chains in which you formerly placed yourselves. Learn to accept the so-called evil and bad as good, and to return good for evil. In this manner, the adjustment can be made with rapidity, and your release from the Wheel of Rebirth made that much sooner.

This is why all esoteric schools teach non-attachment. When man is attached to the things of the personality, he creates karma, and so adds to his long round of future incarnations. Jesus said, "Love your enemies", for he knew that love will achieve balance. He taught men to turn the other cheek, for he knew that nothing comes to us except that which we have earned and that to accept it, is to have done with it. He told man that if he "looketh upon a woman to lust after her, he hath already committed adultery with her in his heart";[1] and in this he gave to the world the Law of Cause and Effect (Karma) for he knew that "as a man thinketh in his heart, so is he."[2]

All great teachers and all schools of Truth have given these concepts to the world in differing terminologies. One day man will awake to the one reality underlying the various word forms, and universal understanding will be characteristic of the human family. To that day do all of us with knowledge look, and for that day do all of us with love lend our efforts.

The students of healing must learn the various types of karma, their nature and manner of manifestation. There are many classifications of karma, but for the present we shall consider that which is of greatest importance to healing. To begin with, I shall use two broad generalizations; after which we shall break each one down into its component parts.

1. Personal karma.

When the intent or will is directed toward a personality or group of personalities, the karma is then considered personal and carries with it much greater consequences than does impersonal karma. Any imposition of will upon another, whether for the so-called good or bad of any individual concerned, is a violation of the basic relationship existing between them and is therefore more

---

[1] Matthew 5: 28
[2] Proverbs 23: 7

difficult to adjust than any other kind of karma.

A man's will is his God-given right, his right to live his life as he wills it, to choose his path in the light of his understanding, and this no disciple ever violates. If man wills to suffer, so be it, and there is nothing the disciple can do but let him exercise his will.

2. Impersonal karma.

When the intent is to create an effect either for the sake of creation itself or for the purpose of investigation, the resultant karma is impersonal and much easier to adjust than any other kind.

When the intent is to reveal Truth, such as in the case of teachers, some creative artists, etc., the karma is considered impersonal.

The student of healing must realize that the kind of karma which manifests as dis-ease, is brought on by the misuse of energy. There are seven types of Ray energy which are the seven expressions of Divinity. These Rays which pour through the etheric network and its system of centers, constitute the sum total of energies apportioned the incarnating entity at any given time, for the purpose of its expression. The entity consciously or unconsciously receives the energy, usually misinterprets its Divine meaning or intended expression, and misdirects it into those channels which constitute the normal habit pattern of thought. The misuse of energy causes energy blocks in the etheric network, a deterioration of the cerebro-nervous system which is so closely related to the etheric network, and disrupts glandular and organic functions.

The seven Ray energies are identified as follows:

1. First Ray of Divine Will and Power

Chapter 3

2. Second Ray of Divine Love-Wisdom

3. Third Ray of Active Intelligence

4. Fourth Ray of Harmony through Conflict

5. Fifth Ray of Concrete Knowledge and Science

6. Sixth Ray of Devotion

7. Seventh Ray of Ceremonial Magic, or Law and Order.

A study of and meditation upon the identification of the Rays will reveal their Divine Intention, thus making it possible for man to become a part of the Universal Divine Expression.

I have stated elsewhere that all dis-ease is the karmic result of harmful emotion. An emotion is caused by the impact of astral energy upon the sensory system of the physical body.

In the light of the above, this means that because the man is polarized in his astral-emotional nature, he receives his quota of energies at that level, misinterprets their meaning as emotion, and misdirects or misuses them as he reacts to their impact.

One other point I should like to bring out at this time is the fact that all dis-ease, whether so-called emotional, mental, or physical, will find its karmic cause in the subconscious. That is to say, it is buried and always emotional. There are no true mental diseases manifesting in the world today, nor will there be until the next root race appears. Man is largely emotional; therefore his illnesses are emotional.

You will note I said the cause is buried. Any realized emotion will manifest karmically as various types of wrong relationship between peoples, but never as disease unless the emotion is held from expression and the individual is frustrated in his attempts to express his feelings.

Lesson 4

Dis-ease of Personal and Impersonal Karma

We shall now break the two general classifications of karma into their component parts for greater understanding of healing methods.

Obviously, the student is more concerned with personal karma, for it plays a much greater role in the manifestation of dis-ease, than does impersonal karma. I shall define some of the differing kinds of personal karma resulting in disease and their manner of manifestation.

1. That which is brought about by misplaced love.

When a mother supposedly so loves a child that she imposes her will upon him to the way of life she deems right for him, she is creating a type of karma which is exceedingly unpleasant and difficult to adjust. The energy of love is actually turned back upon herself, rather than outward toward the child, and it is love of self that is motivating her. She cannot bear to see her child suffer, though it is his right to do so if he chooses. She cannot bear to be disappointed. She cannot bear to be shamed and disgraced by her child's wrong doings, etc.

This misdirection of Second Ray energy creates an energy block between the solar plexus and heart centers, and poisons the astral and etheric bodies. Extreme nervousness, hysteria, heart trouble, and diseases of the blood are the outer manifestation of this type of karma.

To effect a cure of this type of dis-ease, it is first necessary to bring about a change in the direction of Second

Ray energy flowing through the vehicles. That energy must be directed outward toward others; therefore, the self must be eliminated as the chief point of interest. Energy follows thought, and the emotions determine the type of thought entertained by the individual. Love of self stimulates continual thought of self. As a result, the energies of love back up in the etheric network, eventually blocking all expression of love to others.

2. That which is brought about by hate.

This is as destructive as its polar opposite, Divine Love, is constructive. Hate ever destroys its habitat. Its cause is obviously darkness or ignorance, for no man with understanding can entertain hate for anyone or anything. It is actually Second Ray energy manifesting in darkness; or a complete misinterpretation of basic relationships. Hate poisons all the springs of life and manifests as all kinds of so-called mental, emotional, and physical disorders. It will work out in the physical instrument in many ways, according to what is hated and why. Migraine headaches, allergies, pneumonia, many cases of heart ailment, congestion, etc., are manifestations of this kind of karma.

The only cure for this type of dis-ease is the removal of hate and the replacement of love, via the light of understanding.

3. That which is brought about by jealousy, envy, resentment, etc.

This also acts as a poison, since it is closely related to hate, and is another misdirection of Second Ray energy. It will manifest as various allergies, diseases of the bone, slowing down of glandular and organic functions, and particularly does resentment manifest as an arthritic condition.

The cure for this dis-ease is the same as above.

4. That which results from pride.

Pride, another poison and a misdirection of both First Ray and Second Ray energy, will usually manifest as some crippling or disfiguring disease, such as strokes, polio, etc. Many advanced aspirants and some disciples suffer these dis-eases as a result of hidden pride in spiritual attainment. In this case, the thought of the individual is continually directed to himself. He is the center of his universe, and right relationship with his fellows is not established in his awareness.

To effect a cure, a realization of the equality of the many must replace the pride with humility and a sincere desire to serve.

5. That which results from greed.

This is a misdirection of First and Third Ray energy, causing blocks in the throat center and related centers, and manifesting as throat disorders, tumors (often of the brain) and in the case of a power complex, manifesting often as cerebral hemorrhage.

Its cure is the realization of the Law of Supply and Demand and the replacement of the greed with a desire to give—to share with others.

6. That which is brought about by grief.

This is another misdirection of Second Ray energy and one of the chief causes of cancer. That for which the individual longs and grieves is incorporated into the body as criminal cells. Here they multiply and grow as the energy of grief continues to feed them.

Release of that for which one grieves is the only lasting cure.

7. That which is brought about by fear.

This is a misdirection of First Ray energy and is a dominating factor in the man's equipment. It can result in one of two things:

    a. the man loses his strength of will in all or one direction, or

    b. he loses his integrity via an over-development of will in all or one direction.

This will manifest such illnesses as extreme nervous disorder and so-called mental imbalance. He must first realize that he has only himself to fear and face himself if he is to be cured of his difficulty.

8. That which results when the intent to harm is aborted.

If an individual intends to harm another and goes so far as to consciously formulate plans to that effect and is prevented from carrying out his plans, the results will be sudden and violent. Many accidents are caused in this manner.

9. That which results from sex frustration.

This is very common, as all psychologists know, and is the result of almost any buried sex emotion which finds its roots in wrong education, shock, etc. It is a misdirection of the creative energies, causes an energy block in both the sacral and solar plexus centers, and manifests as generative disorders, as well as glandular imbalance and neurosis.

It should also be remembered that very often these buried emotions are a carry-over from former incarnations. When this is the case, their adjustment usually takes much longer and so cure of the dis-ease is more difficult.

We shall now consider the differing kinds of impersonal karma.

1. That which results from wrong aspiration.

This is very common among new disciples. Due to wrong aspiration, the disciple misinterprets the part he is to play in the Plan and so misdirects the energies predominating in his equipment. The results are quite painful, taking the forms of aches and pains which doctors cannot diagnose, and which nothing can cure but right aspiration. In this case the disciple should once again study the rules for disciples, and through that study, plus meditation, arrive at an understanding of right relationship.[1]

2. That which results from wrong motive.

This, too, is a common cause of serious dis-ease among disciples. The wrong motive has been deliberately repressed and the disciple is dishonest with himself. He has not faced the fact that right motive is a growing thing in itself and that it is evolving as the consciousness evolves. This part of himself he refuses to face and so buries it below the threshold of his awareness. Energy blocks arise in the entire center system, causing severe disturbances in the entire organism. Symptoms of this difficulty will often begin with an increased restlessness, nervous irritability, and the manifestation of obstacle after obstacle to service.

The disciple must dare to face all of himself, to examine his motive at each level of the spiral, and to acquire right motive as he progresses upon the path. While he is

---

[1] See: *The Rays and The Initiations*, by Alice A. Bailey, pp. 19 – 24

not satisfied with wrong motive, he does not refuse to recognize it, but instead looks for and transmutes it in the light of his Soul.

3. That which results from a misdirection of energies due to a misinterpretation of the Rays and consequently a mistake in service.

This is common with all new or over-enthusiastic disciples. The dis-ease will manifest in the etheric center system as a depletion of vital life energy. Anemia is often the outer manifestation where the condition is severe.

Discrimination is the answer in this case. Dare to wait until you know, and then act, but do not act upon supposition alone.

4. That which results from experimentation.

Many probationers and aspirants receive scattered bits of knowledge and have not sufficient Wisdom with which to apply that knowledge. As a result, there has been much disease caused by an experimentation with the centers. This is often a tragic thing to observe for the aspirant puts himself through much unnecessary suffering and delays his progress upon the path for long periods of time. Know this: when the time is right for center activation, etc., adequate teaching will reach you which will eliminate any need for trial and error methods of experimentation.

Lesson 5

The Thought-form of Death

The chaotic conditions now manifesting require additional instruction which will aid the disciple in answering the call to service; therefore, I am making available written instruction for all who desire it. This material will be projected as the need of the times calls it forth.[1]

Today we find prominent among the many manifestations a condition of dis-ease. In order to approach this problem with any degree of success, it is necessary first to understand its nature. All disciples recognize the fact that any manifestation is the result of a state of consciousness, and that in order to change the effect one must work on the inner planes with cause. There are many ways of doing this, but the only method concerning disciples at this particular time is that of cure, preferably by absorption. In other words, the disciple does not prevent a potential from manifesting; rather, he meets the manifestation, and by using the art of absorption he effects a cure that, in turn, affects the condition of the whole and reduces the extent of this particular appearance.

This is an extremely important concept to grasp. The manifestation of chaos is a part of the Divine Plan, for only in this manner can karma be balanced. Herein lies the opportunity for balancing the karma of the ages, and beginning the treading of a higher level of the

---

[1] See the sections on "Service", and on "The Subjective Work of Discipleship", in *Applied Wisdom*, by Lucille Cedercrans.

evolutionary path.

The cause of increasing physical disability in the world today we find to be a gigantic race thought-form of death. This thought-form is one of the major factors of the astral illusion veiling reality, the other factor being a sense of separateness. When we break this thought-form down into its component parts we find the following:

1. Fear of death. This, of course, is obvious and does not need a great deal of explanation. Suffice it to say that the greater part of the race entertaining the possibility of extinction creates intense fear, which results in bringing on the conditions resembling the feared end. The transition resulting from dis-ease is unnatural, and its cause lies in the race thought-form of death. The Soul sets about to abstract itself from the form. The personality consciousness intuitively senses the experience confronting it and though totally unaware, it sets out to produce those conditions, as a result of fear, which will eventuate in the passing over. The elimination of this fear will result in perfect health up to the moment of transition and the natural passing over in full waking consciousness.

2. Fear of separation. This fear of loss on the part of loved ones creates in those about to pass over an even greater dread than the one they already entertain. It is telepathically transmitted by the solar plexus into the emotions of the ill one, and his condition obviously becomes worse. The idea of aloneness, of separation, of insecurity, creates within him a type of panic which causes his passing to be extremely difficult.

Disciples should remember, when someone they love is making the transition, that there really is no separation, that the Souls are really one, and that the threads of contact remain intact even after the departure of the physical body. He should let his love follow the one passing to the other side, and eliminate the needless grief of both the deceased and the mourners.

3. Emotions of greed, hate, jealousy, etc. You wonder how this can be: how can strong emotions such as these add to the power of the thought-form of death? Because they are in direct opposition to the principles of life. Perfect consciousness of life expresses itself as right relationship, as the perfection of manifesting energies. Negative emotions create vortices of energy which continually move within the individual ring-pass-not and find no way of expression other than as unpleasant reactions within the personality. As an illustration, resentment creates a Second Ray energy block which manifests as arthritis. All disease not resulting in the transmission of energy, and some that do, finds its karmic cause as harmful emotion. Think on this: it will bring much understanding.

We see this race thought-form so close to the human family today that it all but blots reality from view. It is entertained and given a home by almost every consciousness in human form. As it becomes well established in its home, it controls its environment. Disciples would do well to realize what they are combating. It cannot be confined to any individual or group of individuals, but is rather an entity in itself, feeding off the vital life energy of those who house it. It is, in its sum total, the Dark Forces which disciples hear so much about. Therefore, I would advise you to take this darkness out of the realm of the individual and see it as it is.

You may ask why this thought-form is allowed to manifest. I must answer that it is the lesson that humanity must learn, the obstacle that humanity must overcome, and therefore, it is good when considered from the long range point of view. Disciples are prone, however, to entertain a sense of futility, when they reach this concept without fully understanding it. They forget that they, too, play a part in the evolutionary process and that without them, as without any factor, evolution would not be possible. The obvious course, then, is for disciples to play their part in the overcoming of this darkness in order that light may reach the consciousness of the human race. Disciples are teachers, and that teaching takes many forms, not the least of which is that action revealing to their younger brothers a better way in the light of understanding.[2] This futility of disciples presents a greater problem than that presented by the lower levels of consciousness. You would do well to meditate on this to gain a right perspective.

To come back to the methods of service employed by disciples, we shall consider the work being done by the inner subjective group. They act as a broadcasting station, transmitting into the lower levels of consciousness those energies which precipitate manifestation. The race thought-form is then empowered with greater life force and, seeking expression, it works out in the physical plane in its various phases. The disciples working in the field, the physical world, respond to this activity by meeting with light the darkness given form. They absorb the vibration of the lesser and return it as light, thus illuminating the consciousness involved.

The disciple, to be successful, must have attained a certain illumination himself, and this he must be able to maintain regardless of all that is manifesting about him. This state of consciousness would fill many volumes and yet I find it necessary to elucidate in as few words as possible. This I will endeavor to do with the idea in mind that those truly interested will have ac-

---

[2] See the section on "Teacher Training" in *Applied Wisdom*, by Lucille Cedercrans.

quired sufficient purity of motive to make understanding possible.

In analyzing the illuminated state of consciousness referred to, certain basic concepts stand out, and these I shall attempt to clarify.

1. Perfect consciousness of life. This naturally eliminates all negativity from the aura of the disciple. He is fully conscious of the life principle, recognizing that everything within the Universe is vibratingly alive, that all substance is active thinking substance, impregnated with the Will of God, which works out in the human family as the will-to-be, the Love of God which works out as the consciousness of relationships, and the Intelligent Activity of God, which manifests as the impulse to learn, to know through experience.

Life is that force which animates and permeates all form. It is the essence of form, and without it there would not be anything that is. Nothing is, or indeed ever can be, without life. Life can be neither added to nor taken from, though it may change form many times. This concept is the first prerequisite to perfect consciousness of life. That which we call vital energy is not something vague and illusive, but is rather the essence of our form nature. Its type is available in abundance wherever there is form.

The race, instead of recognizing this fact in nature, identifies itself with the illusion of separation, grief, hate, pain, etc., and apparently dies bit by bit, day by day. Humanity entertains and embraces the illusion of death, becoming unaware of its essential reality. Life, for the moment, seems to be passing them by.

Begin to really live now, by recognizing this principle of life within yourself and those about you. See it as permeating your home and the atmosphere you breathe.

See about you and within yourself a golden aura of vital life energy.

Visualize it as the core of each atom of substance which makes up your bodies and as radiating out to join with this same energy radiating out from every other atom of substance.

See this aura as piercing the veil of illusion to attract to you only perfect manifestations of a perfect life.

Realize this as being true of every one and every thing in or out of form, and you will discover a new world animating the old one about you.

2. Consciousness of perfect relationship. I am presuming that the disciple has attained the realization of the One Soul manifesting in myriad forms and for that reason shall pass on to another not so obvious oneness which many have not as yet realized. This oneness finds itself in the sea of substance. All substance is energy, and is, as we have stated many times, intelligent by nature.

All consciousness, yours and mine, is literally submerged in this ocean of substance, and all of the particles of matter which make up your bodies are in constant motion. They are continually passing in, to, and through your bodies. You may ask what maintains the form? It is the result of a potent thought held by the Soul. Substance adheres to the form, but does so in a passing manner, continually being replaced by substance of a newer and changing vibratory nature. That which is today making up the form of your bodies, was yesterday part of a different form, and will be tomorrow part of yet another form.

Chapter 5

This substance, in constant motion, is intelligent and responds to that thought which is of a steady and strong vibratory frequency, regardless of how right or wrong, relatively speaking, that thought may be. This substance of your form is colored by your thought, and continues to be so until changed by a more positive thought. This thought which is impressed upon substance carries a certain rate of vibration and releases energy activity. The thought, rate of vibration, and energy activity of any particle of substance sweeps other particles of substance into activity, and we see a definite sphere of influence in manifestation.

Subjective work, then, follows this pattern:

1. First the concept to be impressed is realized to the fullest possible extent. This builds the thought-form.

2. The realization is then released into the activity into which you are immediately engaged, thereby being precipitated into that quota of substance within your sphere of influence at any given time.

As an example, we shall consider the hypothetical case of a disciple engaged in the task of digging a ditch and realizing the fact of the Divine Plan in manifestation. The substance within his immediate sphere of influence—that of his own bodies, the air he breathes, the shovel, the earth, the people he contacts—is impressed with his realization of the Divine Plan (as it pertains to the ditch, etc.). The vibratory frequency of the particles of substance is increased, Divine energies are set in motion, and as that substance continues its onward path, becoming incorporated in other forms, it produces effects in those forms and their affairs. This is subjective work on a Universal scale.[3]

---

[3] See the sections on "The Subjective Work of Discipleship", and on "The Internalization Process" in *Applied Wisdom*, by Lucille Cedercrans.

Healing

When we bring this down to a specific act such as healing, the individual concerned is recognized as being a
focal point for the distribution of Divine energies to and
throughout the whole. The disciple then realizes, according to his ability, the perfect consciousness of life,
and the manifestation of that life as the Divine Plan. The
realization is then released into the activity indicated.

Before the disciple can begin to work with the art of
absorption, he must have acquired within himself perfect consciousness of life, the realization of his essential
oneness with all else, perfect love for all, perfect peace,
and absolute stability. I speak of these as being the
ultimate insofar as it is possible to attain them while
still in human form.

Thus established, he attracts to himself all lesser vibra-
tions within his immediate environment and brings
them into harmony within himself. I
give as a symbol of this work the circle
with the dot in the center. The disciple
has found his absolute center, the dot in
the circle, and from there, via the analogy of rhythmic breath, he attracts,
transmutes, releases, and manifests. In
this manner, the periphery expands, ever increasing his
sphere of influence.

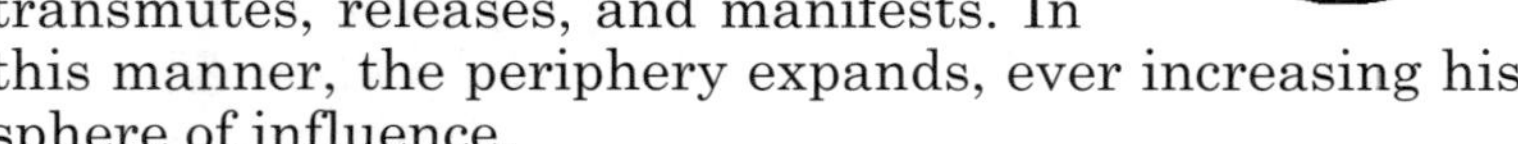

I know of no other words to convey to your present development and understanding this activity, and yet they
are hardly adequate. As a very practical example, I shall
give you the following illustrations:

The disciple becomes aware of his brother's resentment
directed either toward himself or another. If this resentment be directed toward himself, he recognizes first
that nothing comes to anyone that is not his own, regardless of how unfair that resentment may appear. The
disciple knows that in some way he is responsible for it.

It is his creation, possibly originating back in the far past. Thus fortified with this knowledge, he absolves the brother of all blame, and consciously draws the resentment into himself. There he applies to the other's thoughts and emotions his Divine Love, thereby transmuting the resentment into harmless love. This he releases, directing it back to his brother with his blessing. He continues this activity, consciously and positively, thinking and speaking only good of his brother, and eventually the other's attitude will change.

When the disciple can successfully carry out this activity, transmuting all negativity within his environment into its polar opposites of positive love, peace, courage, etc., he has truly found the way of service.

With the imaginative faculty of mind and intuition, this can be made to apply to the physical ills of the human family, but only when the disciple is secure in his center. Ask yourself this question: "Dare I open myself to all of the discord about me, bringing it into myself, to be brought into harmony?" This, of course, necessitates fearlessness, purity of motive, and complete selflessness. Therefore, my brother, until you are sure you are all of these, I would advise you not to use this method, but rather work toward the embodiment of them. Until you have become harmless, this method is not safe.

You may wonder why I have not explained those methods employed by the physical instrument in the art of healing. I say to you they are unimportant. The methods of physical activity utilized by disciples are many and as varied as the energy makeup of the disciples themselves. Each one finds for himself the way, and this he does only after he has attained the state of consciousness of the Divine Healer. The activity then, follows the path of least resistance, taking whatever form is indicated.

Do not forget that the illumined consciousness sees any

activity as being a perfect form for the expression of life. The doctor, the Christian Science practitioner, the laying on of the hands—all of these and many more—become the perfect instruments of healing in accordance with the particular need, insofar as the experience pattern is concerned.

Once again I say to you, do not concern yourselves with the form; rather, set yourselves the task of embodying the illumined consciousness of the Soul. The form the activity takes will then manifest in Divine Law and Order as it becomes instrumental in fulfilling the need.

I have saved for the last of this instruction the ability to visualize, and my reason is obvious. There are so few of you who are as yet capable of benefiting from any explanation of this aspect of healing. However, I find among you one or two who may make immediate use of the instructions, and some of you will, a little later, grow into an understanding of it. Therefore, I shall attempt to set down here the words which will, if meditated and contemplated upon, lead to realization.

You have heard your teachers speak often of the inner eye, and have read many times the words, but have you ever followed the clues given in an attempt to understand the meaning underlying those words?

The Spiritual Eye opens in response to Spiritual Light, just as the physical eyes were a response to physical light. As the Light of the Soul is thrown outward, and all that is, is bathed in this Light, the Spiritual Eye opens to see the form revealed in the light of understanding. Once again I find the words of your language inadequate. The inner eye is literally the Eye of the Soul manifesting in the mind. Here a situation is seen in the light of understanding, all factors being quickly assembled and grasped, the result—Divine application being swift and sure.

Chapter 5

The disciple sees perfection. He looks into the form, seeing the condition of the energies in manifestation, and knowing the perfection of the Soul, he visualizes that perfection in form.

Those of you who have not as yet become conscious of the inner eye would do well to throw the Light of the Soul outward. All of you have a degree of illumined consciousness. Let that illumination reveal that which you see with the physical eye. Learn to focus the inner eye on the world about you, and see it with understanding.

As a step in this direction, gather together the concepts of truth you have acquired into an integrated whole. When you observe a condition of chaos, throw the illumination of that truth outward upon that condition and, in the light of understanding, continue your observation.

The following is a very good seed-thought for meditation:

"The Light of my Soul is thrown outward and all that I see is revealed in its illumination."

Peace Be Unto You—Your Brother In Christ—D.K.

Healing

Meditation – Healing Touch

Please establish your higher alignment directly to the Master D.K., the Master K.H., and the Overshadowing Christ, being receptive to the healing energies being projected through this triangle.

Prepare for meditation please... Focus the consciousness in the cave and identify as the Conscious Soul Incarnate within the instrumentality, visualizing the etheric network and its center system... Take the form of the small golden sun within the cave, radiating light, golden light, into and throughout the etheric body until the etheric body itself radiates light into its environment.

Now visualize the etheric body as it interpenetrates the physical and extends outside—from inside to out... Now realize that this etheric body, this network of lines of force which resemble and underlie the cerebro-nervous system, is highly acceptable to the sense of touch: it is conducive to the sense of touch.

From your focus within the center of the small golden sun, extend, not the consciousness but the awareness, throughout the etheric network, as it interpenetrates the physical and extends out from it, concentrating your attention upon the sense of touch. Endeavor to feel with your etheric the brain and nervous system, which is its outer casing, so to speak... and via the light pouring through the etheric network, increase, just a fraction, the vibratory frequency of the brain and nervous system (which is the outer casing of the etheric)... Now endeavor to feel, via this etheric network, the flesh, blood, bones of the body and again, using the light pouring through the etheric, increase, just a fraction, the vibratory frequency of the flesh, the blood, the bones of the physical instrument...

Let the awareness extend beyond the physical into the atmosphere immediately surrounding the physical body, and with this etheric, feel that atmosphere... Using the light pouring through the etheric, increase, lift the vibratory frequency of the atmosphere immediately surrounding the body...

At the same time, with the etheric, via the etheric extending out from the physical, seek out the four vital energies identified as pranic energies, which nourish and feed, and maintain the health of the physical body... Seek them out and bring them into the instrument via the three heart centers (the higher heart, the heart center, and the lower heart) and the solar plexus center... Bring these energies into the etheric instrument, re-vitalizing, re-energizing it... passing the energies into and through the instrument, back again into the environment...

Relax the focus of attention for just a few moments... pausing between activities—resting...

Now from within the small golden sun in the center of the head, focus the attention to the ajna center and gradually move from the small golden sun to become centered within the ajna center itself... Here realize that this is the center which commands and controls, when consciously utilized, the five energies of lower man...[4]

---

[4] The 5 original lessons on Healing were expanded with the following materials.

Healing

Lesson 6

Developing Your Healing Capacities

All of you should, and are perfectly capable of, developing your healing capacities and techniques. All of you can do this. And all of you should see to it that you give daily attention to developing your healing capacity as disciples, and those techniques which will be naturally your own because you are an individual.

In regard to this, let each one of you make yourself aware of such healing techniques which you should all have, as are generally known through contemplation, meditation, and study. For instance "Esoteric Healing" would be very valuable to all of you in the development of healing techniques and capacities as disciples.[1] Then, through study, through meditation, through contemplation, expand your awareness to include an intuitive knowledge of healing. And thirdly, practice it upon one another. Use it in relationship to your own instrument, to those of your family, to one another, to your children, and so on.

Any one of you, male or female, any one of you within this group, can become, if you will give it your attention, very proficient at healing, particularly the healing of disciples.

There are many techniques. Usually the healer intuits what to do at this time. It is dangerous to give too many

---

[1] *Esoteric Healing*, Volume IV, A Treatise on the Seven Rays, by Alice A. Bailey, Lucis Publishing Company, New York, 1953

general techniques other than those which are basic to the healing art itself.

When you find a great projection of energy from one of the centers, this can be caused by several factors.

First, the life forces may be reversed and draining from the body, which happens very frequently in cases of illness.

Secondly, it may indicate vampires, which you can immediately check. This happens very frequently, particularly in the lower centers. Almost always, if there is a projection of energy through the sacral center for instance, this is a case of vampires, and the entity will probably be in the etheric, and in the nature of an obsession. You simply break the alignment and reverse the flow of energy.

The main element in healing is that of the Soul identified focus. The Soul can heal. In other words, this is natural; a part of the nature of the Soul is to heal. Therefore, the Soul-identified focus is basic. This is really all that is necessary. Once the individual focuses and identifies as the Soul, establishes his higher alignment, and moves with the intent to heal, then he calls to himself all the aid that is available. He receives aid from the Second Ray Ashram; he receives the aid of the Christ; he receives the aid of those Healing Devas that are needed at that particular time.

All disciples, regardless of ray makeup, have the capacity to heal. They will know what to do if they focus their intent to do so. Certainly there are instances when it is better to call in someone else. For instance, if it is someone very close to you, it is better to call another disciple, because the emotional factors can interrupt a healing process.

Master R.:
5-4-52

I would impress upon your minds, first, the fact that no individual can in truth be a healer. No personality is capable of healing. The personality can, however, function as a channel for the energies which pour forth from the source to the condition which is in need of correction.

It is necessary to focus within yourselves the healing energies of the Christ and to transmit them into whatever areas of disease there are in Divine Law and Order.

I shall ask that no person present hold any thought as to specific healing, but that you realize the energies are bringing about Divine Adjustment to the Divine Plan within this group.

I would also ask that each one of you detach now, completely detach from the results of this meeting. Some of you have come here with definite thoughts as to what the results of the meeting are to be. I ask that you eliminate these thoughts from your mind, that you accept now the Will of God as it manifests in your life and affairs.

Master M.:

I am giving you a mantra to be used individually or collectively whenever the appearance of chaos or crisis appears in your life:

> *"May the Divine Will of God manifest in my life and affairs in Divine Law and Order."*

I would suggest that this be used particularly when there is the appearance of difficulty insofar as group relationships are concerned. There has been within some members of this group, criticism of others—an attempt to sit in judgment on another's actions. Those persons should go back to the lessons which they have received, and in the light of the lessons and their own aspiration, dissipate all thoughts of criticism which they have been entertaining.

Master K.H.:

My brothers, that which I would say to you today, I ask you to hold within your hearts and minds during the coming year. This year will bring about many changes in your lives and affairs, both as individuals and as a group.

All that you do and think, do in love and in brotherhood, and know that the Love and Wisdom of your Elder Brothers is yours. Know that all are One in Christ and let that guide you through the year.

The Mahachohan:

I will merely add my vibration and my energies to that which you are receiving. I would give you something about which to think during the coming twelve-month period. I would have you review all that has been given in the lesson material regarding application. Do this in an attempt to discover how you can best express the Divinity which is in each one of you, in service to your brothers. Take every daily activity in which you are normally engaged and observe how much each one is an instrument of service, how into each activity you can pour your love and your light so that others may know that love and be illumined by that light. When you have arrived at a better understanding of application, then I would have you think of precipitation.

Chapter 6

Master D.K.:

I would remind you that it is necessary for each one of you to forgive yourselves before it is possible to forgive others. I would have you remember that it is just as necessary for you to love that which you are as it is for you to love others, that in perfect love no one or no thing is left out. Turn not away from that which you have done or said or felt—love it and right relationship will manifest within each individual as well as within the group.

Realize the great healing power of love. Any manifestation of disease is calling forth your love. Fulfill its need and there will no longer be disease.

Master R.:

Now I have some information which will be both good news as well as instruction for each one of you. This group has been permitted the privilege of receiving a message from the Master Jesus. It will be necessary for the group to raise its vibratory frequency to the range where that message can be contacted and brought through. This will be done during the subjective meeting this evening. I ask each one of you to come to that meeting free of negativity, in aspiration to the Christ.

Master Jesus: (subjective meeting for Wesak Festival):

Blessings, My brothers. Receive My love. Let it cleanse, let it give strength and warmth and light and understanding to all whom you meet upon the path. Be not afraid to speak and act in My name. Whatsoever you shall ask in My name shall be given unto you.

Healing

Master John:

As a disciple engaged in an activity of this type, you are receiving, 24 hours a day, certain of the Ashramic energies; and via your instrument and the centers within your instrument, you channel these energies into the etheric network where they can be received by those members of the human family who relate with them. The disciple or the student undergoes activation within various centers within his etheric body at certain times. The centers in the palms of the hands may be activated. Any one or another or combination of centers in the spine, the head, the feet, throughout the body, will be from time to time activated according to the developing consciousness and the instrumentality. The only attention one should give to this at any specific time is to note it and to endeavor to understand how he can be of service.

This activation of the centers of the hands can mean several things. It can be an indication to open the hand—perhaps you have something to let go of—an indication to hold the hand in blessing and this, of course, symbolizes the attitude of the disciple in his relationships. It does not specifically mean healing.

This is where you can build glamour. Healing comes from the consciousness and the conscious knowledge of the science of healing.

This does not mean that you will not at some future time enter into this field of service. If and when any of you do, it will be as a result of conscious knowledge—not as a result of activity in any part of the form itself. The healer uses form only to convey to the patient the fact that healing is possible to him and that he is healed. The laying on of hands, which is in some respects very old fashioned (if I may use such terminology), is but an outer symbol and one which I should do away with myself very quickly because all healing comes from within the individual's own higher alignment with that which overshadows him.

Master R.:

Meditation—Soul, Brain, and Hand Alignment

Focus as the Conscious Soul Incarnate... Link up with the brain and the hands, becoming conscious of the hands as centers which carry and release, upon direction, the healing energies of the Soul.

Concentrate upon the Soul, brain, and hand alignment... Become conscious of the presence of the healing energies within the hands. Visualize the hands as centers which carry this energy.

As the Soul, with this equipment, realize that you can, through an act of the will, align with the healing aspect of the Ashram of Synthesis, by directing your attention to the Master D.K., the Master K.H., and the office of the Christ, and that, via this higher alignment, you can invoke whatever energies are needed in the healing of any condition of imperfection within the consciousness and its form... that that healing can be directed through the hands to any given destination, in any of the three planes of vibrating matter... in Divine Law and Order and in cooperation with the Soul plan of any individual or group of individuals concerned.

Now, realize that this spiritual healing is a part of the function of discipleship, is a natural activity of the Soul, and that any disciple—regardless of ray makeup or specific field of service—can function in this way if so called upon.

Now again, consider the alignment between Soul, brain,

and hands... recognizing this as part of your service equipment... realizing that, as you give attention to the alignment, and as you use it, so do you become proficient in this function. Sound the OM.

Relax the attention.

Lesson 7

Therapy

You, as disciples, are given ways and means of handling your personality reactions. The reactions will become increasingly evident as group integration takes place. The demonstration of these truths is the hardest part for the personality to "stomach", for at times you must proceed on blind faith to its ultimate conclusion.

Please proceed with group integration, for that is the true power and source of balancing karma in relationship between individuals and between the individual and his subconscious blocks.

In the meantime, focus any problem which you feel you have in direct alignment with the Soul. Move into that magnetic field of the Group Soul within your cave. You have the power of the group at your disposal. Grasp the dark forces within you by deliberately bringing the problem up into the cave, drawing its intent out of the subconscious. Bring it out of the muck and bring its related problems with it up into the ajna center where it can be looked at, acted out, mentally accepted as a problem, then bring it into the Light of the Soul in the cave. Becoming the third party, the observer, deliberately act out the play. There is always a relationship, so there are two or more in your play. You become the audience, seeing the actors perform. Then you take the part of first one and then another of those actors. You become the person or problem involved, taking on the reactions of each, speaking to each, hitting if the play calls for it, screaming or crying, whatever is necessary to feel the emotion of the experience toward the working out of the play to its ultimate conclusion.

See to it, My brothers, for the longer you hold back from looking at truth, the longer you are held a prisoner within the form.

Turn the floodlights on at the end of the play. Bathe the stage in Christ's healing light. Have a curtain call of all of the performers, knowing that each has played his part well.

Release the light into the mental body by moving back out to the ajna center. Look at it, knowing that Truth will set you free. You can even be the editor, writing your reactions to the play.

Move into the heart center and Love the situation, letting it go back into the subconscious as truth.

If another block is inter-related with this one, you know what to do—flood it with the Soul's light using the group magnetic field for the power to rise above the emotion. Take a good hard look at it emotionally and mentally, flood it with the radiance of the Christ, and Love the experience; for it has given you an insight into race-mind consciousness, and you have helped solve humanity's problem through relieving your own. You have helped relieve the congestion within the emotional and mental body of the race through this service to yourself and to your group of brothers.

You have utilized:

First Ray Will to deliberately move the problem up into the light.

Second Ray Love of the Soul to use the Light of the Soul and group magnetic field to surround the play in its ring-pass-not aligned with truth.

Third Ray of Active Intelligence to analyze the play and draw from it its purpose.

Fourth Ray of Harmony through Conflict, acting out the various parts and emotions of the actors.

Fifth Ray of Concrete Knowledge and Science, looking at the results and absorbing the essence back into the subconscious in its true light.

Sixth Ray of Devotion to an Ideal, that the Soul has manifested a healing and that each inter-related particle will be affected with Christ Light.

Seventh Ray of Ceremonial Magic and Divine Law and Order.

Let each one grasp the import of what is taking place, first within his own consciousness, within his own mind, his emotions, and finally within his outer life and affairs. Let him recognize the way in which these happenings are re-adjustments, Divine adjustments, to the manifestation of the Divine Plan for humanity, that humanity which he is, so that with the re-adjustments can come now a reorientation, a recognition and realization of growth, of new abilities, of strength, and of purpose.

To carry this further into the specific: find an emotional disturbance within your sphere of influence and focus what you know upon that situation. You will be making the connection between your own higher Soul consciousness and a specific problem within humanity. Since you have probably already been in the same situation sometime in the past, your resolution will be utmost in your mind. Project your resolution via telepathy into the problem, which is almost certainly one of relationships. Relationships are the way in which we work out our karma. Allow the individual to make up his or her own mind as to what to do, but encircle that individual with love and assurance in Divine Law and Order. Do this as an observer, never getting your emotions involved in the problem. To do that is to take on the karma of the one who is involved with the problem. You know that you have been in a like situation, so give your best effort to first define the problem and then allow the individual to create the path he/she will take. You know you are better qualified to handle the problem, but it is not your problem. It is not you who has to take action.

This is how you carry your wisdom into incarnation. Feel that you have the power and the responsibility to help another without making the actual decision for the type of action to be taken. You work on the inner planes and if asked, of course, take the time and the patience to discuss and show the way, then let it happen. You can control no one, but you can help and observe without being critical.

In the same way, if you are left out of the making of the decision, give the two participants your wisdom and compassion from afar, pouring love and light into the situation and into yourself as well, for you are concerned. Continue to give assurance, knowing all is well, an education is in progress, and the outcome will make right relationship of a bad situation.

If you are the one involved in an unruly situation, focus on the Soul's Divine Intent, not looking for results, but bringing the power of the Soul into manifestation to work it out for you. Give it time, then, to adjust. You are still the observer in the background, letting the Soul's light and love cleanse and purify your being with acceptance of the outcome.

Every one of your relationships has some type of problem. Play like the angel with the magic wand and tap them gently on the top of the head with the light and the wisdom to carry out the scene on their little stage of life in their little drama.

There is one other technique that I shall give you at this time, in relationship to the aura. It can be of use not only to yourselves, but to the overall group life, and to every individual with whom you come in contact.

At least once a day (and you do not have to do this in deep meditation, merely turn your attention to it) align with the Seventh Ray aspect of the Synthetic Ashram and, via that alignment, pull into the aura healing energy which can be called upon by the instrumentality at any time there is need, and which can be directed outward to those who may have need of it, whether they are aware of it or not. It can be directed through any center which corresponds with the area of difficulty which the individual is experiencing. It can be directed through the hands, or simply by thought, as a radiatory action.

Healing

Lesson 8

Diet

You want to diet. The moment you begin to bring the idea into a mental focus you are doing that. You have entered the activity. Now, this is the concept that at this point you need to realize more than any other, for it is this step that you are passing over because it has no reality for you. You want to diet. You think only of the physical idea. The moment you bring the idea into a mental focus, you have entered into the actual thing you want to do. You are doing it.

The first concept to consider at this time, and particularly in relationship to the next step in the internalizing process (the bringing of the idea from its mental focus into an astral activity), is that you, the identified consciousness, must remain polarized in the mental body as you continue to work with this concept.[1] You are going to utilize the astral vehicle. You are going to direct astral force, not become imprisoned within it.

Consider what this means. What is the difference between wanting or desiring to do something—and establishing a mental focus or doing it? The mistake that the human consciousness is prone to as it endeavors to carry out an effort, is to want or desire to do, rather than to do. The moment you enter into the astral body and desire to do that which you intend to do, you drain the power which you have built up in the mental vehicle

---

[1] See also: *Applied Wisdom*—Internalization Process, by Lucille Cedercrans

from the intent so that you no longer have a power potential. Now, this is one of the most difficult concepts to understand and yet one of the most important at this particular step in the process.

You have already entered the activity. You are already doing what you intend to do. Now you are going to have to learn to work with intent, with the energy of decision, with the energy of intent, rather than with the astral desire nature, which wants.

The moment you enter into the astral body and want to do something you are setting up an opposition to the intent you have brought into focus and thereby drain the power from that intent.

Do not get ahead of the concept, remain with it. Do not try to interpret it at this point. Remain with it. You are going to remain mentally polarized in relationship to this intent. Continue to hold the intent focused and see your plan, your thought-form, move from its mental potential into a directed force on astral levels. The only way you can do this is keep yourself above, free of any emotions, in relationship to the intent. It is the power of attraction on astral levels that brings an idea of a plan and energy potential into relationship with substance itself. That magnetic power must be given to the plan itself. When you want, you are, in a sense, taking away from your idea the power, the magnetic attraction, which would bring it into outer manifestation. You are claiming that power, that magnetic attraction, yourself and are being swallowed up within it, possessed by it, obsessed by it.

We will go back to the idea of reducing because this is a good example. It is brought from its mental focus— brought from, not taken out of. The mental focus continues; it is extended down into the frequency of astral force. There it takes on its own desire body. The plan you have created desires to manifest. It desires to come into physical appearance. It has become imbued thereby with the power of manifestation. However, if you enter into a desire yourself (to reduce) you are stealing, in a sense, the power from the thought-form. You are stealing the power to manifest from the thought-form. You are giving power to the opposition, a natural opposition of that thought-form. If you want something, this pre-supposes you do not have it, so that you drain the power immediately from your energy potential. You have destroyed your mental focus, destroyed your mental thought-form completely, the moment you yourself desire that which you have created. For it can come into manifestation only via its own desire, its own magnetic attraction. On astral levels, the connection between the creator and creation must be severed.

Now, you are receiving lessons in pure magic. You are receiving instruction in the creative process.

If you desire the thing you have created, you are holding it attached to you. It cannot possibly move out of the frequency of astral substance. The thing itself, which has been created, must be permitted to build up the attraction. *It* must be given a desire—not you. Once you understand this clearly, you understand the meaning of glamour.

This subject of diet is a very touchy one, and most difficult, because it can be approached from so many different directions. Each of these directions have, in themselves, something of value. Before I go into what you eat, I would like to speak for a few moments regarding the relative purity of the bodies and the degree of purity—wise or desired—at any given time within the bodies.

When the bodies, the etheric and the physical bodies, are maintained at a higher level of purity than would otherwise be the case, and you are, at the same time, living within the physical plane in an etheric network which is relatively impure in relationship to your own bodies, you have the problem of being without immunity to certain conditions. This you should be able to understand very well.

I am referring to the health of the consciousness, to the health of the spirit that indwells that consciousness, and to the health of the instrument which houses them both. This is the basic principle upon which the whole healing science is based, both corrective and preventive.

As you proceed to learn and embody the Wisdom, you naturally lift the frequency of your bodies above the frequency of the environment within which you live. Now you may be able to cleanse and to purify to a certain degree your immediate environment, but only to a certain degree, and you are constantly moving out of that immediate environment and into the environment which surrounds it. Contained within the etheric body or network of the greater environment, which surrounds your immediate environment, are those vibratory frequencies which are the impurities of not only humanity, but the planetary life at this particular level.

You lift the frequencies of your bodies above these impurities and imperfections; and then when you move out of the protection of your immediate environment (relatively free of these frequencies and these impurities), you are, in a sense, attacked again, because your bodies do not have the immunity to withstand these impacts and the effects of those impacts, of the impurities natural to humanity and to the planet.

You must remember that you are incarnate within the etheric body of humanity and your frequencies cannot be lifted, by law, above the point of contact with those within the body of humanity. You can lift your own individual frequencies above those lower frequencies, but a point of contact must be maintained, and it is through this point of contact with the impurities.

You know the law that there is no such thing as a vacuum. Well, you see, in a sense, in relationship to the space around you, you are empty space. You are an instrument which has been cleansed of all impurities, so that, were it a true reflection of the Christ, moving within—if it were to come down within the body of humanity and make contact within the body of humanity, it would become like a vacuum and all of the impurities would rush into the instrumentality. The instrumentality would have nothing, relatively speaking, with which to combat or to resist.

This is one of the basic reasons why the initiate above the third degree incarnates at tremendous sacrifice, because he cannot maintain a vehicle of that degree of purity, which would be natural to his consciousness, within the body of humanity. This is why the Christ cannot walk among men for any prolonged period of time.

The bodies (and we can refer to the planetary bodies, the body of humanity as a whole, and the bodies of the individual) are constantly undergoing the process of lifting in frequency, cleansing, and purification. This is a part of the process of evolution, a part of the redemption of substance, a part, in a sense, of the very saving of the planet itself. It all proceeds under law. It has to be balanced with other factors. Now this is where what you refer to as common sense is of vital importance to you.

As I said, disciples have to make decisions regarding these things. They should bring all of the knowledge that they can possibly acquire to bear upon these decisions. There are ways that a certain amount of these weaknesses can be accounted for. There are measures which can be taken which protect the instrument to a degree. The disciple has to look at all of these different factors and then determine the path he shall take according to the life he lives in the world.

For instance, the disciple who must, of necessity, function in an active social way within the body of humanity—let us say in any one of the world capitals, or in any department of human living where it is necessary for him to do a great deal of entertaining and to be entertained, to eat out, to drink, and so on—it would be death for him insofar as the physical instrument is concerned to achieve any great degree of purity within his etheric and physical bodies.

The monk who lives in a monastery—the lama, and so on—can with relative safety, achieve a high degree of purity and maintain it. If for any reason he finds that he must go out into the world, he has to undergo a tremendous preparation before he can leave his retreat and enter into the world as it is and survive for any length of time.

Now, the average length of time, the average period of time for survival for an instrument, let us say, which has reached the degree of purity that is normal to one leading the monastic life, would be from three to five years. This would be his period of survival in the world with the body that he has created—even with the preparatory work entered into prior to his movement out into the body of humanity—so that in the legends and stories regarding this there is a certain amount of truth.

For you, the problem does become great, because your understanding does not include so many factors which are related here. You have achieved a degree of purity in your bodies, which is certainly unusual insofar as the average humanity is concerned, through your meditation efforts, through (some of you) your diet and the type of lives you lead. Since coming into this area, you have increased that degree of purity simply because you are not in as much contact with the impurities as you were before.

Healing

Chapter 9

Meditation—Group and Centers

Focus the consciousness in the cave and identify as the Conscious Soul Incarnate, linking up with one another.

Via the head center, align with the Master D.K., the Master K.H., and the overshadowing Christ, receiving from the Higher Triangle the healing energies of Divine Love-Wisdom, centering these within the group life.

Add to these energies, as you receive and center them within the group life, Solar and planetary prana—vital life energy. Having anchored, centered, the healing energies of Divine Love-Wisdom as received from the Higher Triangle—the vital life force as received from the Sun and the planet itself—transmit this blend of energies into the substantial forces of the center— centering, then, the three kinds of energy within the mineral, the vegetable, the animal, and the human kingdoms in nature which are focused into the physical property.

Contemplate the concept of healing, first in consciousness, as it applies to consciousness, second, as it applies to relationships and affects the etheric network of the group life, the physical center, surrounding environment, and the world of affairs.

Consider it as it applies to conditions of mind, of emotions, of activity, the Ashramic Group Life, to the substantial forces of the actual physical appearance—the physical property—as being a radiating center of healing, a healing agent functioning within its world of affairs, taking in all of these areas which have been considered.

Contemplate this healing quality and activity radiating from every stone, every blade of grass, every tree, every body, and every unit of consciousness which makes up the center—into and throughout its world of affairs.

Consciously radiate and direct the healing energies— the healing quality, the healing activity—into and throughout all areas within the total group life which are in need of healing. Remember to direct the healing energy into your economy, pouring into it along with the healing energies of the Second Ray, the Solar and planetary prana, revitalizing, re-energizing, and rejuvenating it. Sound the OM.

Now bring the three-fold blend of energies into a focus within your own cave, focused into and through the mental body, the astral body, the etheric body, the etheric center system, physical brain and nervous system, the glandular system, the blood stream, the vital organs, the flesh, skin, the bones, the physical magnetic field. Sound the OM through the whole of the lower alignment.

Relax the attention.

Chapter 10

Meditation—Standard of Health

I am going to project an exercise which you may use to increase the standard of physical health and the vital energy level of the instrument.

Assume the position—both feet on the floor (this can be done in a standing position, preferably out of doors). Calm the emotional body, alert the mind, and focus the consciousness in the ajna center.

Look inward toward the center of the head, visualizing the small golden sun. Permit yourself to be attracted into its center via the magnetic attraction of its light. Focused in the center of the small golden sun, identify as Soul.

Consciously, via an act of the will, radiate the light of the sun, via the brain and nervous system, into and throughout the physical instrument.

Now permit your perception to move into an awareness of living within this etheric light body which interpenetrates the physical body.

Arrive at an interior, inner knowledge of the instrument, the etheric light body. Become aware of its alignment, via the small golden sun, through the head center with the overshadowing spiritual presence of the Christ.

Now via the sounding of the OM, bring the light of that Presence down into the etheric light body within the physical, vivifying and energizing it. OM.

Gradually relax the attention and return to the normal focus.

Now, it is focusing within the etheric light body with that ceremony (which gives substance and which releases into activity) that the formulated plan is carried out.

Chapter 11

Releasing Emotions

(Question was asked about the release of emotion without the realization of what has been released.)

You may never become consciously aware of the cause. Much therapeutic work is being done with disciples below the threshold of their awareness. A new method has been established of bypassing the concrete mind. Since it has been this aspect which has given the greatest trouble in regard to resistance of therapy, we have found a way of linking the soul with the subconscious without utilizing the concrete mind aspect.

Energy projected into the subconscious from the soul results in stimulation and activation of buried thought-forms, releasing buried emotion and gradually eliminating the power of the thought-form to influence the life and affairs of the consciousness. This naturally produces many reactions which are extremely difficult for the individual to understand. It is a much quicker process of therapy than that of analytical therapy. Wherever the karma of a disciple permits, we are using this method. There are many whose karma would not permit this method. No one below the status of a disciple could take advantage of it. The process is established by the Master and carried out under His direction by the soul of the individual concerned. Many members of the World Group are being affected by this method.

This was only established a few months ago and has only been in operation for that period of time. It is proving highly successful, and the time is coming when it will be the one method utilized by disciples.

Healing

I will attempt to clarify somewhat what is taking place with you at this particular time. An old thought-form which previously blocked not only your ability to express love, but your ability to express almost any emotion as well, has been reactivated by this process. The soul has established direct contact with this form and is in the process of devitalizing it. Upon contact with the form there is always, in the beginning, a stimulation due to the life-giving nature of soul energies. However, this stimulation, when watched over and directed by the soul, brings on reactions so violent as to result in emotional release. When the thought-form is depleted of vital life energy, it will disintegrate and the block will disappear without any conscious knowledge on the part of the brain consciousness as to what has taken place. One by one these troublesome blocks will be removed until the disciple will find himself miraculously changed, healed, of many of his difficulties. [1]

---

[1] See also: *The Nature of the Soul*—Lesson 8 Transmutation Technique, by Lucille Cedercrans

Chapter 12

Balancing the Centers

(This technique was never written down, but was taught by Lucille Cedercrans to the group I was attending. It is to be used in a class where one student has an energy block, an over-stimulation in one center (for example, a headache that keeps bouncing around in the head). This would indicate an over-active ajna center where there would be a big bulge in the ajna etheric and hardly any energy in the other centers.)

Pam Dunn Nissen

Ask the one who has a block to sit in a chair so that their back is available to you as you stand.

Make your alignment with the Ashram and the Master of your Ashram. To do this, I align with Master D.K. and visualize his presence coming into my etheric network, and I use his *Presence* to do the healing.

Align the Oversoul of the student (who has a block in one of the centers): Tell the student to align with their own head center, and with those in humanity afflicted with the same dis-ease, so that the student has a flow-through in service.

Rub your hands together, bringing the energy into them. Instruct the rest of the group to visualize the student/patient in an egoic egg (etheric) of golden light for healing and protection.

Place your hands above the student's head center. Aligned with the healing energies of DK, you feel the student's head center by placing your hands, one over the other and moving them up and down (between 1 foot and 6" above the head center) until you contact the energy or vortex of the head center itself. Through your own hands, transmit the energies of that individual from the Ashram into their head center until you "get" a flow.

Keeping the left hand above the head center, move until your right hand is 6 to 12" out from the ajna (you are creating a flow through your hands between the patient's head center via the cave to the ajna).

Move your left hand to the ajna center and your right hand to the patient's throat center. Find the throat center with the right hand by moving it in and out—perhaps 2' to 6"—until you are aware of a good flow between your two hands.

Move the right hand down to the heart center, maintaining the left in the ajna. Go in and out of the etheric, 2' to 6", until you find it and have a steady flow between your two hands.

Leave the left hand in the ajna center and move the right hand down to the solar plexus center; move in and out until you feel the energy pulsating between your two hands.

Move down to the sacral center (repeat).

You have balanced all of the centers and found where the centers are over-energized and where they are almost non-existent. Now, start at the top again—head center to ajna, ajna to throat, ajna to heart, ajna to solar plexus, ajna to sacral. (*Do not stimulate the Kundalini in any way!*).

Now you begin to touch the physical, bringing the energies up from the sacral to the solar plexus to the heart.

From the solar plexus move the energies by touching the body lightly (like touching the physical every inch) up and out the shoulders and down through the arms to the palms.

At this point, have the patient lift their arms and point their palms downward, so you can get under them with your palms facing up, and pull the energies out through the palms by moving your hands close to 2" and then away a foot, until you feel the surge of energies coming out the palms, and then transfer to the fingers and pull the energies out into the etheric.

When satisfied that the energies are moving smoothly from the sacral, up through solar plexus, up through the heart center, into the throat center and out the hands, then start at the hips and work downward.

Starting at the hips in the etheric, with your hands directly across from each other with your energy flowing through your hands, gradually move the energies down the outside of the legs. If you feel any cool spots or very hot spots, go back up past them and gradually work them down the legs (still with your hands on the outside of the legs using your own energy to do this) until the hot or cold is released out the feet and toes into the etheric at least 6". Pull the energies out the bottom of the feet by telling them to lift their feet high enough so that you can get your hands under them.

Go back over the entire etheric network, checking each center again, so that all the centers are equally balanced. When you feel that the work is done, start at the head center and place the patient in a cocoon of golden etheric light from head to toe (etherically) and say,

"In Divine Law and Order."

Both the patient and the server wash their hands with

soap and water to rid yourselves of any black energy, and know that the work has been completed.

(What I have described is not in any of Lucille's published books.

Once I dropped a heavy cookbook on my foot. When I could finally stop hopping around and get control, I proceeded to draw the energy that was still there, hurting like crazy, out the bottom of the foot with the etheric hands. There was not even a bruise the next day.

If we catch an injury right after it happens and proceed to pull the concentration of energy out into the etheric, it heals quickly. If we just let it be, all of our attention is drawn to that spot because it hurts and we damage it even more.

Watch out for any impacts received as registered in your own body because this tells you the group is being impacted and also needs your help. Always lift the energies of the group where it is being impacted, out into the etheric and up to the next center from the impact.

Sometimes you will feel that your etheric is unstable and no particular center is involved. Immediately circle your group in a golden cocoon of light with a blue-white light at the periphery for protection and send the impacting energy back to an unnamed source with Divine Love. This negative energy you use in service to the Christ.

Do not have any individual other than one of the group work on your etheric in this manner. You can do this for yourself with your etheric hands.)

Chapter 13

Meditation

Becoming an Unobstructed Channel

Receptivity to Healing Energies

A few rules and methods of application so that you may from this time on become conscious of the healing energies each one carries and be able to put them to use to a certain degree.

How to Become an Unobstructed Channel:

The disciple first establishes a complete alignment of his three instruments—the physical, the emotional body and the mental body. When this is accomplished and the physical body is relaxed, the emotional body is quiescent and the mental body is alert; then the threefold instrument is focused in the ajna center. Here he completes his alignment with the source and his environment or the subject (whichever it may be) by linking himself with the Soul in the following manner:

He visualizes light in the form of a funnel or tube, extending from above the head (by realizing his contact with unlimited supply) down through the physical, emotional, and mental instrument, into the area which is being given treatment. To make it easier I am going to ask each one of you to think of himself as a funnel or tube, connected at the upper end with the unlimited supply of healing energies, and the other end with the environment.

Healing

The above is to be used for physical illnesses, magnetizing, etc. Visualize the energies as flowing through the hands, etc., the reception of light through the head, passing out through the feet or hands or both. To be used in:

a. Healing.

b. Revitalization.

c. Protection.

For radiation, use the same alignment. Visualize love as radiating from the upper part of the body. To be used for:

a. Healing and transmuting conditions.

b. Radiation of Divine Love-Wisdom.

Radiation should be done often. It is also good to settle one's own emotions.

Receptivity to Healing Energies

I would like to clear up any instrumental difficulty before we proceed with any more intensive meditation work or concentrated esoteric activity. Therefore, I am going to ask you to be receptive throughout the day to healing energies. Be receptive to love, move out among the growing lives, being receptive to the trees and all of the vegetable kingdom, even the grass, to the healing energies which will be focused through them for the healing of the etheric and physical instrument in order to fit it for the work which it has to do now. Let this be the theme of the day, accompanied with joy and a quiet calm serenity, realizing that this is as much a part of your training as is any other work and taking from it, then, a lesson which can be utilized in the future in helping with the healing work of others. In other words, there will be those in the future as there have been in the past, whose need at the moment will be for healing. Moving through this experience yourself, becoming as at-one with the vegetable kingdom, with the devic life of this center today, will place you in a much better position to aid other individuals to do the same thing, the healing power, the healing resources, which have been stored here and which will continue to focus into the vegetable kingdom of this area.

Do not today, then, try to work with them by impressing upon them, but be receptive to them, to their aid, responding primarily with love. At the same time realize that when receiving this healing energy, being affected by it within your own bodies, you are also, then, creating a healing aura about you which will have its effects upon all of those individuals with whom you come into contact. Thus within your own devic structure you are achieving right relationship with the devic lives of the center itself.

Healing

Index

Index

Index

Index

Index

Further Information

For further information on *Healing*, and related courses and materials, see:

www.wisdomimpressions.com

or write to us at:

WisImp@wisdomimpressions.com

or

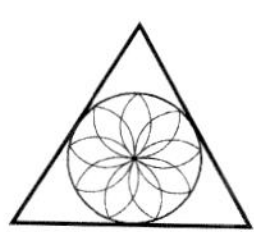 **Wisdom Impressions**
PO Box 130003
Roseville, MN 55113